XTREME RAPTORS

★ ★ ★ ★ ★

VULTURES

BY

S.L. HAMILTON

A&D Xtreme
An imprint of Abdo Publishing | abdopublishing.com

abdopublishing.com

Published by Abdo Publishing, a division of ABDO, PO Box 398166, Minneapolis, Minnesota 55439. Copyright ©2018 by Abdo Consulting Group, Inc. International copyrights reserved in all countries. No part of this book may be reproduced in any form without written permission from the publisher. A&D Xtreme™ is a trademark and logo of Abdo Publishing.

Printed in the United States of America, North Mankato, Minnesota.
022017
052017

Editor: John Hamilton
Graphic Design: Sue Hamilton
Cover Design: Candice Keimig
Cover Photo: iStock
Interior Photos: Alamy-pgs 26 (bottom), 27 (top & bottom), Dreamstime-pg 19; iStock-pgs 2-3, 6, 12-13, 18 & 28; Minden Pictures-pgs 1, 4-5, 7, 8-9, 10-11, 14-15, 16-17, 20-21, 24 (top & bottom), 25, 30-31 & 32; National Geographic-pgs 22-23 & 26 (top); U.S. Fish & Wildlife-pg 29.

Websites
To learn more about Raptors, visit abdobooklinks.com. These links are routinely monitored and updated to provide the most current information available.

Publisher's Cataloging-in-Publication Data

Names: Hamilton, S. L., author.
Title: Vultures / by S. L. Hamilton.
Description: Minneapolis, MN : Abdo Publishing, 2018. | Series: Xtreme raptors
        Includes index.
Identifiers: LCCN 2016962220 |
ISBN 9781532110054 (lib. bdg.) |
        ISBN 9781680787900 (ebook)
Subjects: LCSH: Vultures--Juvenile literature.
Classification: DDC 598.9/4--dc23
LC record available at
http://lccn.loc.gov/2016962220

CONTENTS

VULTURES

Vultures are the cleanup crew of the Earth. These smart scavengers find weak, dying, or dead animals and have themselves a meal.

The word "vulture" comes from the Latin word *vellere*, which means to pluck or tear. Vultures use their sharp, curved beaks to tear the flesh off dead animals. They sometimes even eat the bones. Nothing goes to waste around these birds of prey.

Cape Vulture
(Gyps coprotheres)

XTREME FACT – *Vultures are important to the health of humans. Without the raptors' quick work, poisons from rotting animals can get into water supplies and cause diseases, such as cholera and botulism.*

SPECIES

There are 23 species of vultures. They are divided into New World and Old World vultures. These groupings are based on where the vultures live and how they find food.

NEW WORLD VULTURES

There are 7 species of New World vultures, which include condors. They live in North, Central, and South America. They find their prey using their incredible sense of smell.

The king vulture (*Sarcoramphus papa*) is one of the 7 New World vulture species.

OLD WORLD VULTURES

There are 16 species of Old World vultures, which include griffons and the lammergeier. They live in Europe, Asia, and Africa. They find their prey using their excellent eyesight.

The palm-nut vulture (*Gypohierax angolensis*) is one of the 16 Old World vulture species.

HABITAT & PREY

White-Backed Vulture
(*Gyps africanus*)

Vultures live on all continents except Australia and Antarctica. They make their homes in many areas, including plains, deserts, mountains, grasslands, meadows, forests, and even cities.

Vultures are diurnal, feeding during the day. They can be picky about their meals. Vultures like fresh meat, although a carcass is often not found until it has begun to decay. Vultures prefer to eat dead herbivores, such as cattle and zebras. They will also eat dead reptiles, amphibians, fish, birds, and eggs.

XTREME FACT – A group of feeding vultures is called a wake.

Bearded Vulture or Lammergeier
(Gypaetus barbatus)

EYESIGHT

Old World vultures have incredible eyesight. Because they depend on their vision to find dead animals, these vultures live where there are open areas.

XTREME FACT – An Old World vulture can spot a three-foot (1-m) -long dead animal lying in an open plain from as far away as four miles (6 km).

BEAKS

Like all raptors, a vulture's beak is sharp and curved. It is designed to reach into a dead body and rip off pieces of meat. Vultures eat fast, picking a small animal clean in as little as half an hour. Some vultures even feed on the bones of their prey. They eat until they are almost too full to fly.

Turkey Vulture
(*Cathartes aura*)

XTREME FACT – Turkey vultures have an incredible sense of smell. They have huge, undivided nostrils full of scent receptors that are wired to the large olfactory part of their brains. These raptors can smell the gases given off by dead animals even under trees and leaves. Turkey vultures have helped construction workers find breaks in gas lines.

WINGS & FEATHERS

Vultures
have long wings
and stubby, blunt tails.
They spend a great deal of time
in the air, riding thermals. These
rising columns of warm air allow the
raptors to stay aloft without having
to flap their wings. Vultures' wobbly
flight patterns are a result of waiting
as long as possible to move from
one thermal to another.

XTREME FACT – Vultures have bald or lightly feathered heads. This allows for easy cleanup. Bacteria from a dead meal is killed by the sun's heat on their heads. It's also believed that the baldness may be a way for vultures to control their temperatures. Stretching out their heads and necks helps them cool off, while tucking in lets them stay warmer.

Some vultures soar just feet above the ground, while others remain high in the sky. They often circle slowly, wings extended, sniffing or looking for their next meal.

Bearded Vulture or Lammergeier
(*Gypaetus barbatus*)

LEGS, FEET & TALONS

Vulture legs and feet are designed for walking, hopping, or standing. They have long toes and blunt talons that allow the raptors to steady themselves on their dead prey.

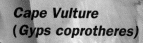

Cape Vulture
(*Gyps coprotheres*)

XTREME FACT – Some vultures have a white substance coating their legs. Vultures "mute," or poop, and allow it to run down their legs. The white substance is uric acid. This powerful chemical kills any bacteria the raptor has come in contact with on dead animals. Their liquid pee and poop also helps cool down vultures on hot days.

SMALLEST VULTURES

The Egyptian vulture is the smallest Old World vulture. These birds of prey are 23 to 28 inches (58-71 cm) in length and weigh 3 to 4.5 pounds (1-2 kg). They have a wingspan of up to 67 inches (170 cm).

The Egyptian vulture *(Neophron percnopterus)* is very smart. This raptor is known to use rocks to break open the eggs it eats.

XTREME FACT – Egyptian vultures are one of the most common symbols found on Egypt's monuments and headdresses. Because of this, the raptors are also called "Pharaoh's chickens."

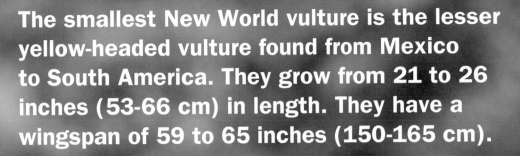

The smallest New World vulture is the lesser yellow-headed vulture found from Mexico to South America. They grow from 21 to 26 inches (53-66 cm) in length. They have a wingspan of 59 to 65 inches (150-165 cm).

The lesser yellow-headed vulture (Cathartes burrovianus) has a weak beak. It depends on bigger vultures to tear open the tough hides of large dead animals.

LARGEST VULTURES

The Andean condor is one of the largest flying land birds in the world. It has a massive wingspan of up to 10.5 feet (3.2 m). Its huge wings allow the raptor to reach heights of more than 4 miles (6.4 km). It can fly as far as 186 miles (300 km) in a single day. This New World vulture makes its home in the Andes Mountains of South America.

Andean Condor
(Vultur gryphus)

Vulture Size Comparison

Turkey Vulture
King Vulture
Andean Condor

XTREME FACT – The Andean Condor has the biggest wingspan of any vulture. However, it is not the biggest in length. It reaches 51 inches (130 cm). The California condor reaches 55 inches (140 cm).

HIGHEST FLIERS

The Ruppell's griffon vulture is the highest flying bird on the planet. It has been tracked to an amazing height of 37,000 feet (11,278 m). This is the height at which commercial airplanes fly. Humans would pass out from lack of oxygen at this height.

Ruppell's
Griffon Vulture
(*Gyps rueppelli*)

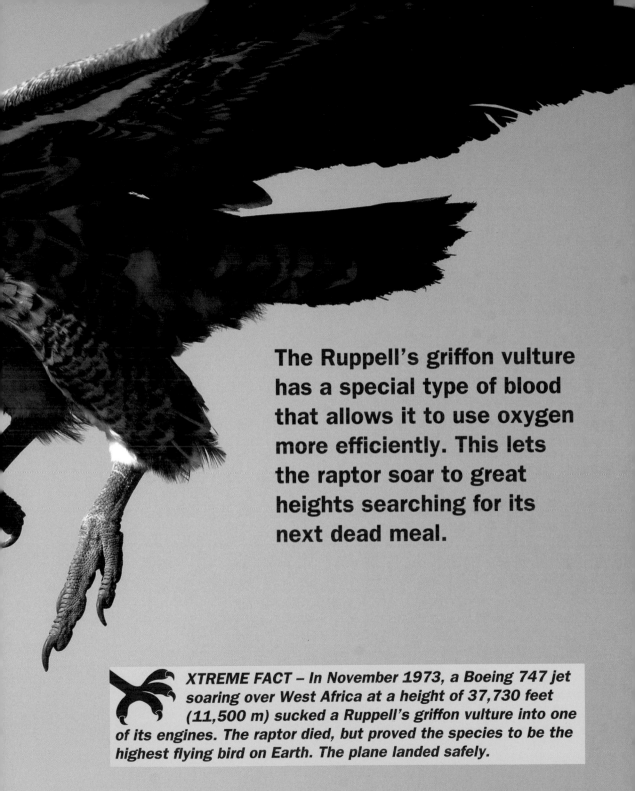

The Ruppell's griffon vulture has a special type of blood that allows it to use oxygen more efficiently. This lets the raptor soar to great heights searching for its next dead meal.

XTREME FACT – In November 1973, a Boeing 747 jet soaring over West Africa at a height of 37,730 feet (11,500 m) sucked a Ruppell's griffon vulture into one of its engines. The raptor died, but proved the species to be the highest flying bird on Earth. The plane landed safely.

Unique Meals

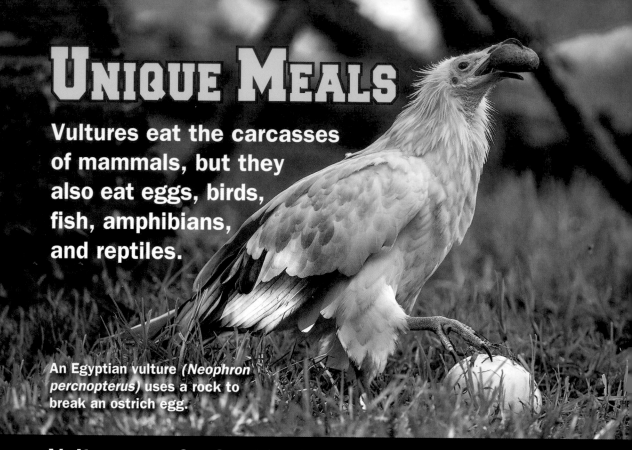

Vultures eat the carcasses of mammals, but they also eat eggs, birds, fish, amphibians, and reptiles.

An Egyptian vulture *(Neophron percnopterus)* uses a rock to break an ostrich egg.

Vultures prefer freshly dead animals, but they have a stomach acid that kills bacteria and allows them to safely eat rotting meat.

An American black vulture *(Coragyps atratus)* eats a dead caiman.

Vulture beaks are not strong enough to break the tough hides of big animals. They may wait for other scavengers to tear into the body first. Or, if no other predators are around, vultures go for the easiest entry points: the dead animal's eyes or butt.

A bearded vulture or lammergeier (*Gypaetus barbatus*) eats a whole leg bone and hoof.

XTREME FACT – Vultures can eat up to 20% of their body weight in one meal. If threatened, they may throw up their meal to fly away faster.

NESTING

A griffon vulture (*Gyps fulvus*) on its nest.

Vultures usually lay one to two eggs each year. Nests are often shallow scrapes in the ground or a bare surface, such as a cliff, cave, or ledge. To protect their nests, vultures throw up semi-digested food around the site. The foul smell keeps predators away.

A six-day-old griffon vulture chick.

XTREME FACT – If vulture vomit gets in the face or eyes of a predator, it will cause stinging pain.

A griffon vulture and month-old chick.

Vulture parents regurgitate food to feed their chicks. A vulture family stays together for several months, even after their chicks "fledge." This is when the young have developed large enough feathers to fly.

A griffon vulture parent feeds a fledgling.

ARE THEY ENDANGERED?

Of the 23 species of vultures, at least 16 are threatened or endangered. They may someday become extinct. Humans have killed or caused a loss of the raptors' habitat. Chemicals found in the environment, and in the carcasses that vultures eat, have resulted in large numbers of raptor deaths.

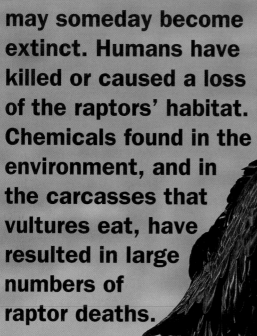

California Condor
(*Gymnogyps californianus*)

People are learning that vultures clean up the environment and reduce diseases spread by dead animals. Captive breeding programs have brought some vulture species back from near extinction. Many people work to keep these important birds of prey from dying out.

California condor #98 with a chick in a nest near Hopper Mountain National Wildlife Refuge in southern California.

XTREME FACT – In 1987, all 22 wild California condors were captured. A captive breeding program began. However, recovery has been slow. By 2014, there were only 228 wild and 193 captive California condors in the world.

GLOSSARY

BACTERIA
Single-celled organisms that multiply rapidly and often cause sickness and sometimes death in humans and animals. Vultures have processes inside and outside their bodies to kill the bacteria that forms on carcasses. This provides a great service to other living things, including people.

BOTULISM
A type of food poisoning caused by bacteria.

CAPTIVE BREEDING
A creature that is not born in the wild.

CARCASS
A dead creature's body.

CHOLERA
A severe intestinal disease transmitted to humans by contaminated food or water. Cholera causes extreme diarrhea and vomiting and can result in death.

DIURNAL
Creatures that are active during the day.

ENDANGERED
When there are so few numbers of a plant or animal, it is close to becoming extinct. See also "threatened."

HABITAT
The natural home of a living thing.

HERBIVORES
Animals that eat plants as food, such as cows.

OLFACTORY
Olfactory refers to a sense of smell. New World vultures have a large olfactory area in their brains.

SPECIES
A group of plants or animals that are related to one another. They look alike and may produce offspring.

THREATENED
When a plant or animal is at risk of extinction in the very near future. See also "Endangered."

INDEX